Digital Declutter in One Weekend

Clear the clutter, reclaim your time, in just one weekend.

Written by

ERIC LEBOUTHILLIER

AcraSolution | 2025 1st Edition
www.acrasolution.com

Preface

Who this book is for

This book is written for anyone who feels **overwhelmed by digital clutter** and wants a fast, practical reset. If you've ever…

- Opened your inbox to hundreds (or thousands) of unread emails,
- Felt stressed by constant pings, dings, and notifications,
- Scrolled endlessly through apps without purpose,
- Or wasted time searching for lost files in a digital mess —

…then this guide is for you.
It's perfect for **busy professionals, students, entrepreneurs, parents, and everyday tech users** who want to simplify their digital world and reclaim peace of mind — without spending months on complicated systems.

What to expect from this book

Digital Declutter in One Weekend gives you a **step-by-step plan** to clean up your digital life in just two days. Inside, you'll find:

- **A Weekend Reset Blueprint**: clear goals, simple rules, and a mindset shift to make digital decluttering doable.
- **Inbox Zero Made Simple**: strategies to slash email overload, filter messages, and unsubscribe in bulk.
- **Phone Freedom**: how to audit your apps, silence distractions, and create a minimalist home screen.
- **File & Cloud Organization**: easy systems to tidy your desktop, documents, and cloud storage once and for all.
- **Social Media Detox**: clean up your feeds, set healthy limits, and make platforms work for you.
- **Sustainable Habits**: daily and weekly rituals that keep your digital life organized long after the weekend.

By the end, you'll walk away with **a lighter inbox, a calmer phone, and a clearer mind** — plus simple routines to keep your digital world clutter-free for good.

LEGAL DISCLAIMER

This publication is intended solely for informational and educational purposes. It does not constitute legal, financial, medical, or professional advice. The content is not a substitute for consultation with qualified experts or licensed professionals in the relevant fields.

Portions of this work have been created or assisted by artificial intelligence (AI) tools. While every reasonable effort has been made to review, fact-check, and edit the content for clarity and accuracy, AI-generated information may occasionally contain errors, omissions, or generalized statements. The author and publisher do not guarantee the accuracy, completeness, or reliability of the information provided.

Readers are strongly encouraged to seek independent advice tailored to their personal circumstances from qualified legal, financial, healthcare, or compliance professionals before making decisions or taking action based on this content.

References to specific products, services, companies, websites, or technologies do not imply endorsement or affiliation unless explicitly stated. All trademarks and brand names mentioned remain the property of their respective owners.

The author and publisher disclaim any liability, loss, or risk incurred directly or indirectly from the use or misuse of this publication. This includes, but is not limited to, damages of any kind — including incidental, special, or consequential — arising out of the reliance on the material presented.

All references to laws, regulations, security standards, or industry guidelines are intended for general awareness only and may not reflect the most current legal developments. This publication is not intended to create, and receipt does not constitute, a client relationship with the author, publisher, or any affiliated entity.

By reading, accessing, or applying the content in this publication, you agree to do so at your own risk. If you do not accept these terms, you are advised to discontinue use of this material immediately.

Table of Contents

INTRODUCTION

Why Digital Clutter Is Holding You Back

Our devices promise freedom. With a single tap, we can connect with friends across the world, access limitless knowledge, or spark a new idea. Yet for many of us, the digital tools designed to simplify life have quietly become sources of overwhelm. Instead of clarity, our phones and laptops often deliver distraction, scattered focus, and a sense of being permanently "behind." This is the hidden cost of digital clutter.

Unlike physical clutter—piles of paper, messy closets, or overstuffed garages—digital clutter is less visible. It hides in our inboxes, notification panels, cloud storage, and even in the dozens of open tabs we tell ourselves we'll return to "later." But just because it doesn't occupy physical space doesn't mean it's harmless. In fact, digital clutter can be more draining than the physical kind because it occupies the most precious space we have: our attention.

The Weight You Don't See

Research in cognitive psychology shows that every piece of unresolved information—an unanswered email, a neglected reminder, an unread message—creates a small mental burden known as the Zeigarnik effect. Our brains keep these "open loops" active, subtly demanding energy until the task is resolved. Now multiply that by the hundreds of alerts, drafts, files, and feeds we encounter daily. The result isn't just a busy device; it's a restless mind.

Consider how often you pick up your phone with one intention—say, to reply to a message—only to find yourself, twenty minutes later, scrolling through unrelated apps, unsure why you even unlocked the screen in the first place. That momentary lapse is not a personal weakness. It is the architecture of digital clutter hijacking your focus.

The Hidden Costs of Always-On Living

Digital clutter doesn't just consume attention; it erodes well-being. Notifications interrupt deep work, making it harder to concentrate long enough to solve problems or generate creative ideas. Studies show it takes an average of 23 minutes to refocus after a single interruption. Imagine the compound effect of dozens of pings in a single day.

On an emotional level, digital clutter fosters a low-level anxiety we often mistake for "normal stress." A crowded inbox can feel like an accusation: *You are behind.* An overflowing to-do app whispers: *You'll never catch up.* Even unused apps, sitting idle on your phone's home screen, carry silent weight—the weight of intentions never fulfilled.

The Illusion of Productivity

One of the most dangerous aspects of digital clutter is that it masquerades as productivity. We equate busyness with progress, checking notifications as if each one brings us closer to our goals. But the reality is the opposite: constant micro-distractions fragment our attention, leaving us with less capacity for meaningful work.

Imagine trying to write a chapter of a book while someone taps you on the shoulder every two minutes. That's what digital clutter does—it turns your focus into confetti. You may feel busy, but busyness is not the same as progress.

Why a Reset Matters Now

Our digital lives are unlikely to slow down on their own. Every year, new platforms, apps, and services compete for our attention. If we don't take control, we become passengers in a system designed to keep us reactive instead of intentional. A digital declutter is not about rejecting technology—it is about reclaiming agency.

By consciously clearing the noise, we create room for clarity, focus, and meaningful connection. Just as tidying a messy room brings relief, decluttering your digital world can bring a lightness you may not have realized you were missing.

The Takeaway

Digital clutter is not a small annoyance—it is a silent barrier to growth. It drains focus, fuels anxiety, and keeps you locked in cycles of distraction. But the good news is this: just as clutter is created through small, daily choices, it can also be cleared with intentional steps. A single weekend dedicated to digital declutter can reset your relationship with technology and unlock a more focused, purposeful way of living.

CHAPTER 1

The Weekend Reset Mindset

Identifying Clutter Triggers

You cannot declutter what you cannot see. Digital clutter often disguises itself as "normal life," blending into the rhythm of daily habits until it feels invisible. The first step in reclaiming control is awareness: recognizing the situations, tools, and thought patterns that generate clutter in the first place. When you can identify your triggers, you shift from reacting to technology to consciously shaping your relationship with it.

The Notification Trap

For many, clutter begins with a single buzz. A new message, a breaking news alert, a sale notification—each one promises importance, but most are trivial. Psychologists call this "variable reward," the same principle that makes slot machines addictive.

Sometimes the notification is meaningful; often it's not. But because you can't predict which, you feel compelled to check every time.

The result is twofold: clutter accumulates in the form of hundreds of unread alerts, and your focus fragments as your brain constantly shifts tasks. The trigger is not just the notification itself, but the *fear of missing out* on what it might contain.

Strategy: Audit your notifications. Which apps truly require your immediate attention? For most people, the answer is only messaging and calendar reminders. Silence the rest. By removing the trigger, you prevent clutter before it starts.

The Overflowing Inbox

Email is another major trigger. Unlike paper mail, which arrives once a day, email flows continuously, creating a sense of urgency. A full inbox isn't just an organizational issue—it's a psychological weight. Every unopened message becomes an "open loop," demanding mental energy.

Take the example of a professional who starts their day intending to tackle a major project but decides to "quickly" check email. Two hours later, they're still replying, sorting, and clicking links. The trigger here isn't the work itself; it's the belief that productivity begins with inbox zero.

Strategy: Redefine your relationship with email. Set fixed times to check it, and filter incoming messages so that only what truly matters reaches your attention. Treat email like physical mail— something you sort intentionally, not constantly.

The Endless Scroll

Social media apps are engineered to trigger engagement through infinite feeds. The "bottomless bowl" effect, studied in behavioral psychology, shows that when people eat from a self-refilling bowl, they consume far more than when eating from a normal plate. Social feeds operate the same way: there is no natural stopping point.

What begins as a quick check can stretch into an hour of unconscious scrolling. The clutter accumulates not only in your feed but also in your mental space, filling your head with fragmented information you didn't choose to consume. The trigger is boredom or the brief discomfort of an empty moment.

Strategy: Redesign your environment. Move social apps off your home screen, or set time boundaries using built-in screen tools. Replace the trigger with healthier defaults, such as reading or stretching during short breaks.

Digital Hoarding

Another subtle trigger is the fear of letting go. We keep thousands of photos, dozens of apps, and countless files "just in case." This digital hoarding is often driven by a scarcity mindset—the belief that deleting something means losing opportunity or security.

But the reality is the opposite: hoarding clutters your device and mind, making it harder to find what truly matters. Think of the person who scrolls endlessly through thousands of screenshots to locate a single important image. The trigger here is anxiety about permanence.

Strategy: Reframe deletion as curation. Instead of asking, *What if I need this someday?* ask, *Does this serve me now?* Trust that truly valuable items will resurface when needed, and that technology provides more reliable storage systems than your overflowing camera roll.

Emotional Triggers

Not all clutter stems from technology itself. Often, the trigger is emotional. We reach for our phones when we're anxious, lonely, or procrastinating. The device becomes a buffer against discomfort. But instead of resolving the underlying feeling, it layers on digital clutter—more tabs, more notifications, more half-finished tasks.

Strategy: Practice a pause. The next time you reach for your phone, ask yourself: *What am I feeling right now?* If it's boredom, maybe a short walk would serve better. If it's stress, a five-minute breathing exercise could bring more relief than opening another app. Awareness of emotional triggers gives you power to choose differently.

The Takeaway

Clutter doesn't appear by accident. It's the product of triggers—external alerts, endless feeds, emotional patterns—that nudge us into reactive behaviors. By identifying your personal triggers, you transform the process of digital declutter from guesswork into strategy. The goal is not to eliminate technology but to remove the unconscious cues that create noise, leaving behind tools that genuinely support your focus and growth.

Goal Setting — Designing Your Digital Declutter

Decluttering without direction is like cleaning a room with no idea of how you want to use the space afterward. You might throw away a few items, shuffle things around, and feel temporarily lighter—but the clutter will return because you never defined a purpose. The same is true for your digital life. To create lasting change, you need more than good intentions. You need goals.

Goal setting is not about adding pressure or rigid rules. It's about clarifying what you want technology to do for you—and what you will no longer allow it to do. When your digital environment aligns with your values, every tool becomes a support system instead of a distraction.

Why Goals Matter in Digital Decluttering

A weekend spent deleting apps and unsubscribing from emails may feel productive, but without clear goals, it's easy to slip back into old habits. Research on behavior change shows that people are far more likely to sustain new practices when they tie them to a compelling "why." In other words, you need to know what your digital declutter is serving.

Ask yourself: Do you want to focus better on your studies or work? Do you want more presence in relationships? Do you want to reduce anxiety caused by constant notifications? Each of these requires different strategies. Your goals provide the filter that tells you which changes are essential and which are optional.

From Vague Intentions to Clear Targets

"I want to use my phone less" is not a goal—it's a wish. A real goal is specific, measurable, and time-bound. For example:

- *I will limit social media use to 30 minutes a day for the next month.*
- *I will reduce my inbox to fewer than 50 messages by Sunday evening.*
- *I will delete all unused apps from my phone this weekend.*

These kinds of targets transform decluttering from a vague idea into a concrete project. They give you benchmarks to celebrate and prevent the process from feeling endless.

Aligning Goals with Values

Effective goals are not just about numbers; they connect to what matters most to you. If family is a priority, your goal might be to keep your phone in another room during meals. If career growth is your focus, you may set a goal to create a distraction-free desktop for deep work.

Consider the story of Maya, a graduate student who found herself overwhelmed by constant group chat pings. Her goal was not simply to mute notifications; it was to reclaim mental space for thesis writing. By reframing her clutter-clearing around her deeper value—academic progress—she found the motivation to stick with new boundaries.

Setting Goals You Can Actually Keep

Unrealistic goals can sabotage your declutter before it begins. Deleting every app, unsubscribing from every list, and achieving inbox zero in a single day may sound appealing, but it can create burnout. Behavioral science emphasizes the power of "small wins." When you succeed in modest, achievable goals, your brain releases dopamine, reinforcing the new behavior and building momentum.

A more sustainable approach is to set tiered goals:

1. **Quick Wins** — Delete five unused apps, archive old files, silence one distracting notification.
2. **Moderate Challenges** — Clean up your inbox, organize your photo library, set social media limits.
3. **Stretch Goals** — Redesign your digital workspace, commit to device-free hours, or overhaul your cloud storage.

This layered structure keeps you moving forward without overwhelming you.

Writing Your Digital Mission Statement

One powerful way to set goals is to create a simple mission statement for your digital life. Write a sentence or two that defines how you want technology to serve you. For example:

- *"I use technology to learn, create, and connect meaningfully—not to distract myself."*
- *"My digital environment supports my health, relationships, and focus."*

Keep this statement visible—on a sticky note by your desk, or as your phone's lock screen. When you face clutter triggers, it serves as a reminder of your deeper intention.

Tracking Progress Without Adding More Clutter

Ironically, the tools we use to track goals can sometimes become clutter themselves. The solution is simplicity. You don't need a dozen apps to monitor your digital habits. A small journal, a whiteboard, or even the notes app on your phone can serve as your tracking system.

Check in daily: Did you meet your goal? If not, what triggered the slip? This reflection builds self-awareness, allowing you to adjust instead of abandoning the process.

The Takeaway

Goal setting is the anchor of a successful digital declutter. Without it, your efforts risk becoming temporary fixes. With it, every choice you make—from silencing notifications to deleting old files— becomes purposeful. Clear goals give you direction, connect your actions to your values, and ensure that your digital reset is not just about less clutter, but about more freedom.

Weekend Rules — Setting the Boundaries for Your Reset

A digital declutter in one weekend is less about speed and more about intensity. You are not casually tidying your phone while watching TV. You are making a focused, intentional reset. To succeed, you need rules—simple guardrails that keep you from slipping back into old patterns during the process. Think of these as your "ground rules" for the weekend: they provide structure, reduce decision fatigue, and help you stay committed when distractions try to creep in.

Rule 1: Treat It Like a Real Project

A common mistake is treating digital decluttering as a side task you'll "fit in" around errands or entertainment. That approach guarantees half-done results. Instead, block off this weekend as if you were preparing for an exam, launching a product, or moving houses. Put it on your calendar. Tell people close to you. When you take it seriously, you set the tone for real transformation.

Practical step: Choose your starting time and ending time for each day. For example: *Saturday 9 a.m. to 5 p.m., Sunday 10 a.m. to 3 p.m.* This structure creates urgency and accountability.

Rule 2: No Multitasking

Digital clutter thrives in distraction. If you attempt to declutter your inbox while binge-watching a series or scrolling social media, you'll end up doing neither effectively. Research shows that multitasking reduces efficiency by up to 40% because your brain must constantly "switch gears."

Practical step: During your declutter blocks, turn off notifications, close unrelated tabs, and silence your phone (unless the phone itself is what you're decluttering). The rule is simple: *only one task at a time.*

Rule 3: Decide Once, Don't Revisit

Clutter often survives because of indecision. We tell ourselves: *I'll delete this later* or *I'll decide when I need it.* The weekend reset is not about postponing decisions—it's about making them once and moving forward.

Practical step: Apply the "two-second rule." If you hesitate over a file, app, or email for more than two seconds, ask: *Does this serve me now?* If the answer is no, delete or archive. Trust the process.

Rule 4: Work in Focused Sprints

Staring at screens for hours can drain you quickly. The goal is to declutter with energy, not exhaustion. That's why your weekend should be structured around focused sprints rather than marathons.

Practical step: Use the 50/10 method—50 minutes of focused decluttering, followed by a 10-minute break. This balances efficiency with recovery, keeping your mind sharp across the weekend.

Rule 5: No New Clutter Allowed

It makes little sense to clear out hundreds of emails while subscribing to three new newsletters. During your reset, you must close the "leaks" that create clutter. Otherwise, you'll be bailing water out of a sinking boat.

Practical step: Pause all non-essential notifications, avoid installing new apps, and resist signing up for services that promise to "help" but usually add noise. This rule is about holding the line.

Rule 6: Prioritize Progress Over Perfection

You won't achieve digital perfection in one weekend. And you don't need to. The goal is momentum, not flawlessness. Perfectionism often paralyzes—making you overthink whether a folder structure is "just right" or whether every photo needs labeling. That's not the point. The point is to reduce clutter significantly and create a system that works better than what you had.

Practical step: If you're stuck between perfect organization and simply "better than before," always choose progress. You can refine later.

Rule 7: Protect Your Energy

Decluttering is not only a mental task but also an emotional one. Deleting old photos, archiving years of emails, or unsubscribing from once-beloved projects can stir up nostalgia, regret, or even anxiety. Recognize that these feelings are normal—and temporary.

Practical step: Keep water nearby, move your body during breaks, and remind yourself why you're doing this. Pair the process with small rewards (a walk outside, a favorite snack) to keep motivation high.

Rule 8: End with a Ritual of Closure

A weekend reset deserves a proper ending. Without closure, it's easy for clutter to creep back. By marking the end of the weekend with a simple ritual, you solidify the progress you've made.

Practical step: Write down three changes you want to maintain beyond the weekend, or read your digital mission statement aloud. Celebrate the accomplishment—because you've just reclaimed control of your digital life.

The Takeaway

Rules are not restrictions—they are the structure that makes freedom possible. By following these weekend principles, you transform your digital declutter from a vague wish into a focused, high-impact project. With clear boundaries, you won't waste energy deciding how to work. You'll know exactly what to do, how to do it, and when to stop. The rules create discipline; the discipline creates results.

CHAPTER 2

Tame the Inbox

Inbox Zero — Reclaiming Control of Your Email

For many people, email is the single largest source of digital clutter. Unlike physical clutter, it doesn't pile up on your desk in plain sight, yet the mental weight is often heavier. A crowded inbox whispers: *You're behind. You missed something. You should be responding.* Each unread message is an open loop, tugging at your attention until it's resolved.

Achieving **Inbox Zero** is not about obsessively checking email every five minutes. It's about creating a system where your inbox is no longer a chaotic storage bin but a streamlined tool that serves you. When your inbox is clear, you feel lighter, sharper, and far more in control.

Why Inbox Zero Matters

Research shows that incomplete tasks occupy mental bandwidth, even when you're not working on them—a phenomenon called the **Zeigarnik effect**. An inbox with 1,200 unread emails is essentially 1,200 tiny mental weights, quietly draining your focus.

Consider the case of Daniel, a project manager. Every time he opened his inbox, he felt a spike of anxiety. He wasn't afraid of the work itself but of the mountain of unresolved messages waiting. After implementing Inbox Zero, he reported that checking email no longer felt like "walking into a storm." The difference wasn't just organizational—it was emotional.

The Three Roles of Email

Part of the problem is that most people use their inbox as:

1. A **to-do list**
2. A **storage archive**
3. A **communication channel**

This overload makes it impossible to stay on top of messages. The first rule of Inbox Zero is this: **your inbox is only a temporary holding area, not a workspace.** Its job is to capture incoming information until you decide what to do with it. Nothing should *live* there.

The Five-Action System

To clear your inbox effectively, you need a repeatable decision-making framework. Productivity expert Merlin Mann, who coined the term "Inbox Zero," recommends processing each email with one of five actions:

1. **Delete** — Most emails can go straight to the trash. If it's irrelevant, let it go.

2. **Delegate** — If someone else can handle it, forward it immediately. Don't keep it as a burden.
3. **Respond** — If it takes less than two minutes, reply right away.
4. **Defer** — If it requires more time, move it to a task manager or calendar, then archive the email.
5. **Do** — If it's actionable and quick, complete the task now.

Notice the word "process," not "check." You're not grazing through messages—you're making decisive choices.

The Weekend Inbox Reset

Here's how to achieve Inbox Zero during your declutter weekend:

1. **Set a Clear Goal** — For example: *"By Sunday evening, I will have fewer than 50 messages in my inbox."*
2. **Batch Delete** — Start by mass-deleting or archiving promotional emails, newsletters, and notifications. Use your search bar to filter by sender (e.g., "Facebook," "Amazon") and clear hundreds at once.
3. **Unsubscribe Ruthlessly** — If you wouldn't notice this newsletter missing from your life, unsubscribe. Each "maybe later" subscription is a leak in your system.
4. **Sort Remaining Emails with the Five-Actions System** — Work through your inbox in sprints, making quick decisions. Don't overthink—clarity comes from momentum.
5. **Create Folders or Labels Only Where Necessary** — Avoid overcomplicating with dozens of categories. A few core folders (e.g., *Action Required, Waiting, Reference*) are enough.

By the end of this process, your inbox will no longer feel like an overwhelming swamp but a clean, functional space.

Staying at Zero

Clearing your inbox once is powerful. Keeping it there is transformational. The key is developing habits that prevent reaccumulation.

- **Check at set times only** — For example, 11 a.m. and 4 p.m. This eliminates the reactive cycle of constant checking.
- **Use filters** — Have newsletters bypass your inbox and land in a "Read Later" folder. Let priority messages rise to the top.
- **End each day with a mini-reset** — Spend five minutes clearing or archiving messages so the next day begins fresh.

The Takeaway

Inbox Zero is not about perfection—it's about liberation. It's about ending the silent stress of thousands of unread messages and reclaiming email as a tool instead of a trap. When your inbox is empty, your mind is clear. You can focus on what matters most, confident that nothing important is buried under the noise.

Inbox Zero is not a chore. It's a gateway—to more clarity, more focus, and more growth.

Filters and Folders — Building an Email System That Runs Itself

Clearing your inbox once is powerful. But staying at inbox zero requires more than willpower—it requires a system. Without one, emails creep back in, notifications multiply, and soon you're back to square one. The secret is automation: filters and folders that quietly organize your messages so you don't have to.

Think of it like a postal service. Imagine if all your physical mail arrived in a single giant box, with no separation between bills, ads, and personal letters. That's what an unfiltered inbox is: chaotic and exhausting. Filters and folders are your mail sorters, making sure everything goes to the right place before you even open it.

Why Relying on Folders Alone Fails

Many people try to stay organized by creating dozens of folders and manually dragging emails into them. While well-intentioned, this approach often backfires. You waste time deciding where each email belongs, and soon the folders themselves become cluttered.

The principle is simple: **let filters do the heavy lifting.** Folders are destinations, but filters are the rules that move messages automatically. When combined, they turn your inbox from a dumping ground into a self-sustaining system.

The Core Folders You Actually Need

You don't need twenty folders for every possible scenario. A lean system is easier to maintain. Here are the only essential categories most people require:

1. **Action Required** — For emails that need a response or follow-up but take more than two minutes.
2. **Waiting** — For items you've delegated or are awaiting a reply.
3. **Reference** — For useful information you may need later (receipts, instructions, records).
4. **Read Later** — For newsletters, updates, or non-urgent material.

That's it. Four folders are enough to cover nearly every situation. Simplicity reduces friction and keeps your system sustainable.

Filters: Your Silent Assistant

Filters (sometimes called rules) automatically sort incoming mail based on criteria you define: sender, subject, keywords, or even attachments. With a few filters, you can reduce inbox noise dramatically.

Here are some high-impact examples:

- **Newsletters & Promotions** — Filter by the word "unsubscribe" and send all such emails directly to *Read Later*.
- **Receipts & Confirmations** — Filter keywords like "receipt," "confirmation," or "invoice" into *Reference.*
- **VIP Senders** — Star or label messages from your boss, clients, or family so they always stand out.
- **Social Notifications** — Direct all Facebook, Instagram, or LinkedIn emails to *Read Later* or straight to trash.

Once filters are set, you don't waste mental energy deciding what's urgent versus noise—the system decides for you.

How to Set Up Filters Quickly

1. **Search First** — Use your inbox search bar to group similar emails (e.g., "from:LinkedIn").
2. **Create Rule** — Most email clients allow you to create a rule directly from that search.
3. **Choose Action** — Decide whether to skip the inbox, apply a label, move to a folder, or mark as important.
4. **Apply to Existing Emails** — Many services allow you to retroactively apply filters, instantly clearing hundreds of old messages.

This process may take 30–60 minutes to set up once, but it saves you hundreds of micro-decisions every week.

Avoid the Trap of Over-Organizing

It's tempting to create a folder for every project, year, or topic. But over-organization leads to clutter disguised as neatness. You shouldn't need to think, *"Did I file that under Work > Clients > 2023 > Proposals or Work > Clients > Invoices?"*

The test is simple: if you can't remember the system instantly, it's too complicated. Remember, modern email search is powerful—far more efficient than digging through subfolders. Use folders sparingly and filters strategically.

The Weekend Filter Reset

During your declutter weekend, dedicate one focused session to setting up filters. Start with your top three email categories (e.g., newsletters, receipts, notifications). Create filters that handle those automatically. Then, as new types of clutter appear in future weeks, add filters gradually. Over time, your inbox becomes a streamlined space where only truly important messages land.

The Takeaway

Filters and folders are not about control for control's sake—they're about freedom. When your inbox organizes itself, you're free from constant triage. Instead of battling a flood of messages, you're calmly processing a few important ones. The system does the sorting, leaving you with the clarity and energy to focus on what matters.

A clear inbox is not a one-time achievement; it's a habit supported by structure. With the right filters and a few essential folders, you build an email environment that practically runs itself.

Unsubscribe Blitz — Cutting Off the Noise at the Source

Inbox Zero is useless if tomorrow you wake up to fifty new promotional emails, updates, and newsletters you never read. That's why one of the most powerful parts of your digital declutter weekend is the **Unsubscribe Blitz**—a concentrated effort to stop clutter at its source.

Every unwanted email you tolerate is an open invitation for more. By removing these inputs, you're not just cleaning today's inbox— you're preventing tomorrow's flood.

Why Unsubscribing Matters

Most people underestimate the drain of low-value emails. Even if you ignore them, they still demand mental energy: scanning the subject line, deciding whether to open, delete, or archive. Multiply that by dozens per day, and you're spending hours each month on messages you didn't even want.

This is called **decision fatigue**—the mental exhaustion that comes from making repeated trivial decisions. By unsubscribing, you remove those micro-decisions entirely.

The Blitz Approach

An Unsubscribe Blitz is not a slow trickle of unsubscribing "whenever you notice." That rarely works. The blitz is a **dedicated session** where you clear out subscriptions in bulk. The goal is speed and finality.

Step 1: Hunt the "Unsubscribe" Link
Open your inbox, search for the word *unsubscribe*, and you'll see nearly every newsletter, promotion, or update you've ever received. This single search creates a target list for decluttering.

Step 2: Unsubscribe Aggressively
Go through the results and unsubscribe without hesitation. If you've ignored ten emails from a sender already, you will ignore the next ten. Let it go.

Step 3: Delete the History
After unsubscribing, mass-delete the backlog from that sender. Don't let old clutter linger.

When to Use Filters Instead

Not every subscription is pure noise. Some you may want, but not in your primary inbox. For example:

- Store discounts you use occasionally
- Newsletters you enjoy but don't need daily
- Community updates that are nice to skim but not urgent

For these, set a **filter** to automatically move them into a *Read Later* folder. This way, they're available when you want them, but invisible when you don't.

Resist the "Resubscribe Trap"

Many people declutter their inbox only to sign up for new mailing lists weeks later—sometimes out of habit, sometimes out of curiosity. Before you hand over your email again, pause. Ask:

- Will I actually read this?
- Can I access this information elsewhere (like a website or podcast)?
- Does this add value daily, or just noise?

By applying this filter upfront, you prevent clutter before it starts.

Tools That Help

If you want to speed things up, there are services like **Unroll.Me**, **Clean Email**, or built-in unsubscribe tools in Gmail and Outlook that batch-manage subscriptions. But remember: automation is only effective if you make decisive choices. Tools can help you process, but you must commit to cutting the noise.

The Takeaway

The Unsubscribe Blitz is about reclaiming ownership of your attention. Every subscription you eliminate is one less tug on your focus tomorrow. Inbox Zero clears the backlog; the Blitz ensures it doesn't return.

Think of it this way: digital declutter isn't just about sweeping the floor—it's about fixing the leak in the ceiling. Stop the noise at the source, and you'll find your inbox stays clear with far less effort.

CHAPTER 3

Streamline Your Phone

App Audit — Reclaiming Your Phone, One Icon at a Time

Your phone should be a tool, not a trap. Yet for most people, it has quietly become both a workplace and a casino, carrying productivity apps alongside infinite-scroll entertainment. An **App Audit** is the process of separating what helps you from what hijacks you. By doing so, you strip away friction, reduce temptation, and create a device that actually supports your goals.

Why Too Many Apps Hurt You

Every app is not just an icon—it's an invitation. Even unused apps take up mental space. They clutter your home screen, send background notifications, and demand updates. Psychologists call this **cognitive load**: the more options you see, the harder it becomes to focus on the ones that matter.

Consider this: if your phone has 120 apps, even finding the one you need requires extra scanning and decision-making. By contrast, when only essential tools remain, your device feels lighter, faster, and more intentional.

Step 1: Identify the Three Categories

When auditing, every app falls into one of three categories:

1. **Essential** — Tools you use daily that align with your values (messaging, maps, calendar, banking).
2. **Useful but Non-Essential** — Apps you use occasionally, but that don't require prime placement (ride-sharing, travel, health tracking).
3. **Distractions** — Apps designed to capture attention rather than serve a clear purpose (endless feeds, games, compulsive shopping).

The key is honesty. An app might be entertaining, but if it leaves you drained more often than fulfilled, it belongs in category three.

Step 2: Delete Without Hesitation

Digital clutter thrives on "just in case" thinking: *I might use this someday.* In reality, most people use only a fraction of their installed apps. If you haven't opened it in a month, delete it. The app store is not going anywhere—you can always reinstall if you truly need it later.

Step 3: Silence the Survivors

For the apps you keep, turn off unnecessary notifications. Constant pings from news apps, shopping deals, or social media do not deserve your attention. Keep alerts only for true essentials— messages, calls, calendar events. This transforms your phone from a slot machine into a calm workspace.

Step 4: Redesign Your Home Screen

Once you've decluttered, restructure your home screen to reflect your priorities. Place only **high-value apps** on the first page. Move distracting but still-necessary apps into folders or secondary screens. This design acts as an environmental nudge: the tools you want are easy to reach, while the temptations require extra effort.

For example, imagine unlocking your phone and seeing only:

- Calendar
- Messaging
- Notes
- Maps
- Camera

Everything else is tucked away. The result is less friction and less chance of getting sidetracked.

Step 5: Audit Regularly

An App Audit is not a one-time purge. New apps will creep in— through curiosity, convenience, or recommendation. That's normal. What matters is keeping a recurring schedule. Once a month, scan your device: which apps did you not use? Which ones drained more time than they deserved? Remove them.

Think of it like spring cleaning, but monthly. Light maintenance prevents the buildup that leads to another weekend of heavy decluttering.

The Psychological Shift

Deleting apps isn't just about saving storage—it's about identity. Every app you keep reflects a choice about who you are and how you spend your time. When you remove distractions, you send yourself a signal: *I prioritize clarity over noise. I choose intention over impulse.* That shift, repeated daily as you interact with your streamlined device, strengthens your sense of control.

The Takeaway

An App Audit is less about minimalism and more about alignment. The apps on your phone should serve your values, not erode them. By deleting distractions, silencing survivors, and redesigning your digital environment, you transform your phone from a source of stress into a partner in growth.

The audit is not about living with less—it's about living with what matters.

Notifications Reset — Taking Back Your Attention

Notifications were invented to be helpful. A calendar alert keeps you on schedule, a message from family deserves your attention, and a reminder about an upcoming meeting is genuinely useful. But somewhere along the way, notifications multiplied beyond necessity. Now, for most people, they function less as assistants and more as interruptions.

A **Notifications Reset** is about flipping the script: instead of being at the mercy of every app that wants your attention, you choose which alerts truly deserve it. This single shift can reduce stress, extend focus, and instantly make your digital life quieter.

The Cost of Constant Pings

Each time your phone buzzes, your brain shifts gears. Research on task-switching shows that even small interruptions can cost **up to 23 minutes** of lost focus before you return to deep work. Multiply that by dozens of alerts a day, and it's no wonder many people feel constantly "busy" yet unproductive.

Notifications also exploit the brain's **dopamine system**. Each ping could mean something exciting or important, which keeps you hooked. But like slot machines, most of the time, the payoff is trivial: a sale on shoes, a social like, or a weather update you didn't ask for.

Step 1: Audit Every Notification

Start by reviewing your notification settings app by app. On most phones, you'll find this under *Settings > Notifications*. Ask:

- Does this alert help me act immediately?
- Is it tied to something essential (work, family, safety)?
- Or is it just noise dressed up as urgency?

Most alerts fall into the third category. They're not urgent—they're distractions.

Step 2: Keep Only the Essentials

At minimum, most people only need:

- Calls and text messages
- Calendar events or reminders
- Direct work communication (e.g., Slack, Teams) if required professionally

Everything else—news, promotions, social updates, app badges—can be silenced. You'll still see them when you open the app, but they'll no longer interrupt your flow.

Step 3: Redesign How Alerts Appear

Not all notifications need to buzz, vibrate, or light up your screen. Adjust the *style* of alerts so they're less intrusive. For example:

- Silent notifications for non-urgent updates
- No lock-screen previews (so your phone doesn't become a billboard of distractions)
- Badge counts turned off—those little red circles are psychological bait designed to pull you in

This way, even the alerts you keep don't hijack your focus.

Step 4: Schedule Notification Checkpoints

Instead of letting notifications drip-feed throughout the day, batch them. Many devices now allow **summary notifications**—a feature that delivers alerts at scheduled times (e.g., 12 p.m. and 6 p.m.). This transforms notifications from interruptions into information sessions you control.

Step 5: Separate Work and Personal

One overlooked source of stress is the blending of work and personal alerts on the same device. If possible, separate channels:

- Use a dedicated work profile or app container.
- Silence work notifications after hours.
- Keep personal messages separate from professional ones.

This separation reinforces boundaries that protect your mental space.

The Psychological Payoff

When you reduce notifications, two things happen:

1. **Calm returns.** You're no longer on edge, waiting for the next ping.
2. **Focus strengthens.** You can finally sustain attention long enough to do deep, meaningful work.

People who implement a full reset often describe it as *"like someone turned down the volume on my life."* The noise stops, and space for clarity appears.

The Takeaway

Notifications are not neutral—they're engineered to capture attention. A Notifications Reset puts you back in control. By silencing non-essentials, redesigning alert styles, and batching when you receive them, you stop living reactively. Instead of your phone dictating your day, you decide when and how you engage.

This reset is not about missing out—it's about finally showing up fully for what matters.

Minimalist Home Screen — Designing Calm Into Your Device

Every time you unlock your phone, you step into an environment that shapes your behavior. A cluttered home screen filled with dozens of apps, flashing badges, and bright icons pulls your attention in multiple directions before you even remember why you picked up the phone. This isn't accidental—your device is designed to compete for your focus.

A **Minimalist Home Screen** flips that design. Instead of chaos, you create clarity. Instead of temptation, you create intention. By curating what you see first, you turn your phone into a gateway for purpose, not distraction.

Why the Home Screen Matters

Research on **choice architecture** shows that the way options are presented influences the decisions we make. Grocery stores put candy near the checkout for a reason: visibility drives impulse. Your home screen works the same way. If Instagram or TikTok sits front and center, you'll open them without thinking.

A minimalist layout reduces **decision fatigue** and prevents unconscious taps. It ensures that the first thing you see serves your goals, not someone else's.

Step 1: Start With a Blank Canvas

Delete everything from your home screen. Yes—everything. Most phones allow you to remove icons without uninstalling the app. This creates a moment of clarity: an empty screen, free of noise. From here, you'll rebuild intentionally.

Step 2: Add Only Essentials

Now, add back only the apps that support your daily priorities. For most people, this means:

- **Communication:** Messages, phone, email (if you truly need instant access).
- **Organization:** Calendar, notes, task manager.
- **Navigation:** Maps, transit, or weather.
- **Utility:** Camera, banking, or health app.

The test is simple: if you don't use it every day for meaningful action, it doesn't belong on the first screen.

Step 3: Push Distractions Out of Sight

Move time-draining apps (social media, games, shopping) into folders on the second or third screen. The extra friction of swiping and tapping forces a moment of awareness: *Do I really want to open this right now?* That pause is often enough to break the autopilot.

Step 4: Neutralize Visual Noise

Colors and badges are designed to attract your eye. Minimize this pull by:

- Turning off app badge counts.
- Grouping apps by function (not by color or brand).
- Using widgets selectively—for information that adds clarity (calendar, to-do list), not clutter (news feeds).

The goal is a screen that feels calm, not crowded.

Step 5: Consider the Wallpaper Effect

Even your background influences behavior. A loud or busy wallpaper adds visual noise; a simple, calming image reinforces focus. Some people use neutral colors, others choose motivational text or even a blank background. The key is intention—what do you want to feel when you open your phone?

The Psychological Shift

When you create a minimalist home screen, you're not just reorganizing apps—you're reshaping habits. Every time you unlock your phone, you're greeted with space instead of noise, tools instead of temptations. Users often report that this single change reduces screen time dramatically, because it breaks the unconscious loop of opening apps "just because they're there."

The Takeaway

Your home screen is prime real estate. Treat it like it matters. By stripping it down to essentials, pushing distractions out of sight, and designing for calm, you create a phone that supports focus rather than fractures it.

A minimalist home screen is not about austerity—it's about alignment. It's a daily reminder that your attention is yours to design.

CHAPTER 4

Organize Your Files & Cloud

Desktop Cleanup — Creating a Workspace That Works

For many people, the computer desktop has become a digital junk drawer. Random files, half-finished projects, screenshots, and shortcuts cover the screen until it feels overwhelming. Every time you log in, you're greeted not with clarity, but with chaos.

A **Desktop Cleanup** is about reclaiming this space as a true workspace—one that signals focus, not distraction. Just as a clean desk encourages deep work, a clear digital desktop sets the tone for productivity.

Why the Desktop Matters

The desktop is your computer's front door. It's the first thing you see when you start working, and like a cluttered entryway at home, it creates a mood. Research in environmental psychology shows that visual clutter reduces concentration and increases stress. The more scattered your desktop looks, the harder it is to feel organized.

Step 1: Sweep It Clean

Start by moving everything on your desktop into a temporary folder called **"Desktop Dump"**. This gives you instant clarity—a blank surface to work from—while keeping files safe for sorting later. Just seeing the empty space creates a psychological reset.

Step 2: Redefine the Desktop's Purpose

The desktop is not storage. It's a launchpad. Its purpose is to provide quick access to the few things you need daily—not to hold every file you've ever touched. From now on, treat it as a **transit zone**, not a permanent home.

Step 3: Create a Simple Structure

Instead of scattering files, set up 3–4 broad, high-level folders on your desktop or (better) in your Documents folder. Examples:

- **Work**
- **Personal**
- **Reference**
- **Archive**

Keep it simple. The fewer decisions you need to make about where something belongs, the more sustainable the system will be.

Step 4: Use Shortcuts, Not Storage

For apps or documents you truly use daily, create shortcuts on the desktop or in the taskbar/dock. But resist the urge to keep *everything* there. Shortcuts should represent action, not clutter.

Step 5: Automate Where Possible

Your computer can organize for you if you set rules:

- On Mac, use **Stacks** to automatically group files by type (images, PDFs, docs).
- On Windows, use **Quick Access** folders and sort by date or category.
- Use cloud sync (Google Drive, iCloud, OneDrive) so files don't linger on the desktop indefinitely.

Step 6: Schedule Recurring Cleanups

Desktop clutter creeps back unless you build maintenance into your routine. End each week by sweeping the desktop—moving finished items into their proper folders or archive. Think of it as digital housekeeping: five minutes now prevents chaos later.

The Psychological Payoff

When you sit down to a clean desktop, your brain receives a cue: *this is a focused space.* Instead of being reminded of 27 half-finished tasks, you start from calm. Many professionals find their stress drops immediately once their desktop is no longer shouting at them with clutter.

The Takeaway

Your desktop is not a filing cabinet. It's a workspace, and like any good workspace, it should be clear, functional, and aligned with your priorities. By redefining its purpose, simplifying its structure, and maintaining it weekly, you create a computer environment that encourages productivity instead of anxiety.

A clear desktop is more than aesthetic—it's strategic. It tells your mind: *You are ready to focus.*

Naming Systems — The Key to Finding Anything Fast

Decluttering removes noise, but organization ensures the noise doesn't return. One of the simplest yet most powerful tools for long-term digital clarity is a **consistent naming system**. Files, folders, and documents often become cluttered not because of volume, but because of inconsistency. A clear naming convention transforms your digital space from a messy archive into a system you can navigate instantly.

Why Names Matter

Search functions are powerful, but they only work if you can remember what you're looking for. If your files are called *"Final Draft.docx"*, *"Final Draft V2.docx"*, and *"Final Draft V2 (final) (edited).docx"*, search won't help—you'll still waste time guessing.

Psychologists studying **cognitive offloading** note that our brains are poor at remembering arbitrary labels. A naming system is external memory: it reduces decision fatigue, speeds retrieval, and keeps projects moving without friction.

Principles of a Good Naming System

A strong naming convention should be:

1. **Consistent** — The same format every time.
2. **Descriptive** — Clear enough that you know what's inside without opening it.

3. **Scannable** — Easy to sort chronologically or alphabetically.
4. **Future-Proof** — Still makes sense months or years later.

Step 1: Use Dates Intelligently

Dates are the backbone of most effective systems. Always format them as **YYYY-MM-DD** (e.g., `2025-09-12_Report.docx`). Why? Because this keeps files in true chronological order. Contrast that with random formats like `9-12-25` or `SeptReport`, which break sorting and create confusion.

Examples:

- `2025-01-15_ClientMeetingNotes.docx`
- `2025-03-01_Invoice_Johnson.pdf`

Step 2: Add Clear Descriptors

A good file name answers three questions:

- **What is it?** (Report, Invoice, Draft)
- **Who/For whom is it?** (Client name, project name)
- **When was it created or updated?** (Date stamp)

For example: `2025-05-10_ProjectAlpha_Proposal_V1.docx` is far clearer than `Proposal.docx`.

Step 3: Handle Versions Cleanly

Version chaos is a classic form of digital clutter. Instead of piling on words like *"final final"*, use a clean numbering system:

- `V1`, `V2`, `V3` for drafts
- `Final` only once—when it's truly final

Example:

- `2025-04-02_BrandGuide_V1.docx`
- `2025-04-07_BrandGuide_V2.docx`
- `2025-04-15_BrandGuide_Final.pdf`

Step 4: Standardize Folder Names

Folders benefit from the same rules. Keep them simple, consistent, and descriptive. Examples:

- `Work_Projects`
- `Personal_Finances`
- `Photos_2025`

Avoid vague names like *"Stuff"* or *"Misc."* These become digital dumping grounds where files vanish.

Step 5: Apply Across Devices

Your naming system should be universal: the same on your desktop, cloud storage, and phone. This reduces friction and prevents the frustration of remembering different rules for different platforms.

Step 6: Build Habits, Not Just Structures

The system only works if you use it daily. The rule: **name it right the first time.** Renaming later almost never happens. It takes seconds to type a clear, consistent name upfront, but those seconds save hours of future searching.

The Psychological Payoff

A consistent naming system creates a sense of order and mastery. Instead of dreading the question *"Where did I save that file?"*, you know exactly how to find it. The relief is not just practical but emotional—you trust your system, which frees mental energy for higher-value work.

The Takeaway

Digital clutter is not just about too much—it's about disorder. A naming system eliminates that disorder by creating clarity and predictability. With consistent, descriptive, and scannable names, you transform chaos into order and make your files work for you instead of against you.

This is the difference between drowning in data and navigating it with confidence.

Cloud Sync Habits — Making Your Digital World Seamless

Decluttering your files is powerful, but if they're scattered across multiple devices and services, the clutter creeps back. A forgotten draft on your laptop, half your photos on your phone, and receipts buried in email create hidden friction. The solution isn't more storage—it's better **cloud sync habits**. When used intentionally, cloud sync makes your digital life seamless: every important file accessible, up to date, and backed up.

Why Cloud Sync Matters

Cloud storage isn't just about space. It's about reducing **fragmentation**—the stress of wondering where something is. Studies in cognitive psychology show that uncertainty increases mental load; when you don't know where to look, your brain has to keep track of multiple possibilities. A strong sync habit removes that uncertainty. You always know where your files live.

Step 1: Choose One Primary Cloud Service

Many people end up with Dropbox, Google Drive, iCloud, OneDrive, and random app-specific storage—all active at once. This redundancy creates confusion and duplication. The first rule of cloud clarity: **pick one primary service** and commit to it.

Criteria for choosing:

- **Integration** — Works smoothly with your devices.
- **Reliability** — Secure, with strong uptime.
- **Ease of Use** — Searchable and intuitive.
- **Space** — Enough storage for your needs, with room to grow.

Once chosen, migrate essential files into this single ecosystem. Keep backups elsewhere, but let one service be your "home base."

Step 2: Mirror the Same Folder Structure

Your cloud system should match the folder system on your computer. If your desktop has `Work`, `Personal`, and `Reference`, your cloud should mirror it exactly. This prevents the classic mistake of treating the cloud as a dumping ground. Consistency is key: the same paths on every device.

Step 3: Sync Automatically, Not Manually

Manual uploads invite forgetfulness. Instead, set automatic sync for:

- **Documents** — Sync your main folders (Work, Personal, Archive).
- **Photos** — Turn on automatic camera uploads. This ensures your images are backed up without thought.
- **Notes & Tasks** — Use apps that sync natively across devices (e.g., Notion, Evernote, Apple Notes, Todoist).

The less effort required, the more reliable the system becomes.

Step 4: Separate Active vs. Archive

Clutter creeps in when your cloud holds everything forever. Use two clear zones:

- **Active** — Current projects, ongoing documents.
- **Archive** — Completed work, old receipts, reference material.

This division keeps your daily workspace lean while still preserving access to past material.

Step 5: Clean as You Go

A cloud is not infinite; it just feels that way. Without habits, it turns into a digital landfill. Build maintenance into your workflow:

- Delete duplicates immediately when you spot them.
- Move finished files into Archive once a project ends.
- Once a month, review your cloud storage for clutter.

Small, consistent actions prevent the overwhelming backlog.

Step 6: Sync Across Devices Mindfully

Just because you *can* sync everything everywhere doesn't mean you should. For example, you may not need thousands of archived photos on your work laptop. Choose what belongs where. Keep essentials universal, but let heavier archives stay cloud-only to avoid slowing devices.

Step 7: Ensure Backup Redundancy

Sync is not the same as backup. If something is deleted on one device, it often disappears from all synced devices. Protect against this by:

- Enabling **version history** in your cloud service.
- Keeping a secondary backup (external drive or another cloud).
- Testing recovery once in a while so you know the system works.

The Psychological Payoff

When your files are synced and structured, you stop wasting energy asking, *"Where did I save that?"* Instead, you trust the system. That trust creates calm, and calm creates focus. People who build strong cloud sync habits report not only fewer lost files, but also a greater sense of mental order.

The Takeaway

Cloud sync is not about hoarding—it's about harmony. By choosing one primary service, mirroring your structure, and building consistent habits, you create a seamless digital environment. Files live where you expect them, photos back up automatically, and your devices feel like extensions of each other instead of scattered islands.

Strong cloud sync habits don't just save time; they protect peace of mind.

CHAPTER 5

Social Media Detox

Declutter Feeds — Taking Back Control of What You Consume

Your feeds—social media timelines, news apps, YouTube recommendations, even podcasts—are not neutral. They are carefully engineered to maximize your time spent scrolling, not your growth. The result is often a diet of information that's endless but unsatisfying: fragmented headlines, shallow updates, and an overwhelming sense of being "plugged in" yet undernourished.

Decluttering feeds is about shifting from **algorithmic default** to **intentional design**. Instead of being pulled into whatever the feed serves you, you choose what enters your mind. This is one of the most powerful ways to reduce digital noise and reclaim focus.

Why Feeds Become Cluttered

Modern feeds are driven by algorithms trained to optimize one thing: attention. The more you linger on sensational or distracting content, the more of it you're shown. Over time, this creates a warped mirror of your interests—one that exaggerates curiosity into obsession.

The problem isn't just wasted time. Research shows that information overload increases stress, lowers memory retention, and creates decision fatigue. When your feeds are cluttered, you aren't choosing your inputs—they're choosing you.

Step 1: Identify Your "Junk Feeds"

Not all feeds are harmful. Some genuinely inform, educate, or inspire. The problem is the **junk feeds**:

- Social media timelines designed for infinite scroll
- "Recommended for you" carousels (e.g., YouTube, TikTok)
- News apps pushing endless breaking stories
- Shopping feeds with "suggested items"

These feeds add noise without delivering real value. Recognizing them is the first step.

Step 2: Unfollow Aggressively

Every account you follow is an open channel into your mind. If it doesn't add value, cut it. That means:

- Unfollow brands pushing ads disguised as posts.
- Unfollow influencers who spark comparison instead of growth.
- Unfollow news sources that repeat the same cycle of outrage.

The test: after seeing this account's content, do you feel informed, inspired, or distracted? If it's the latter, unfollow.

Step 3: Use "Mute" and "Unsubscribe" Wisely

Some accounts belong to people you can't unfollow for social reasons. That's where **mute** comes in. Muting keeps your feed clean without burning bridges.

The same applies to podcasts, newsletters, and YouTube channels. Subscribing is easy—unsubscribing feels harder. But every subscription you drop is a commitment to less noise.

Step 4: Replace Algorithms with Intentional Sources

Instead of letting algorithms decide, create your own information diet. Practical options:

- **Newsletters or RSS feeds** from trusted writers (instead of clickbait headlines).
- **Playlists** you curate for YouTube or podcasts (instead of autoplay suggestions).
- **Books and long-form articles** saved in a reading app (instead of fragmented threads).

The difference is huge: you move from consumption by default to consumption by design.

Step 5: Redesign Access Points

The easiest way to declutter feeds is to reduce how often you see them.

- Remove addictive apps from your home screen.
- Log out after each session so access requires intention.
- Use "feed blockers" or extensions (like News Feed Eradicator) that replace infinite scroll with a blank screen or a motivational quote.

Every extra layer of friction makes mindless scrolling less likely.

Step 6: Set Boundaries for Engagement

Even valuable feeds can become overwhelming if unchecked. Set clear limits:

- Allocate a fixed daily window (e.g., 20 minutes of news in the morning).
- Turn off autoplay features.
- Use timers to end sessions before they stretch into hours.

Boundaries convert feeds from endless streams into intentional check-ins.

The Psychological Payoff

When you declutter feeds, you notice the difference immediately:

- **Less noise.** Your mind feels calmer without constant updates.
- **More depth.** You replace fragments with richer, longer-form ideas.
- **Higher focus.** Without the pull of infinite scroll, you regain hours each day for meaningful work or rest.

Decluttering feeds doesn't mean ignoring the world. It means choosing what deserves your attention and filtering out what doesn't.

The Takeaway

Your feeds are either tools for growth or pipelines of distraction. By unfollowing aggressively, muting wisely, and replacing algorithms with intentional sources, you reclaim the single most valuable resource you have: your attention.

Decluttered feeds don't just change what you see online—they change how you think, how you feel, and ultimately, how you live.

Set Time Limits — Building Boundaries That Stick

Most apps are designed without natural stopping points. News feeds refresh endlessly, social platforms scroll forever, and streaming services autoplay the next episode before you can even reach the remote. Without limits, hours vanish unnoticed.

Setting time limits is about restoring natural boundaries in a digital world that has erased them. Instead of relying on willpower in the moment, you create systems that prevent excess before it begins.

Why Willpower Isn't Enough

Behavioral psychology makes this clear: in environments designed to exploit attention, self-control is fragile. Just as it's harder to stop eating from a bottomless bowl, it's harder to stop scrolling an infinite feed. The answer is not more discipline—it's better design. Time limits act as external guardrails, reducing the cognitive load of deciding when to stop.

Step 1: Use Built-in Tools

Most smartphones now come with **digital wellbeing features** (iOS Screen Time, Android Digital Wellbeing). These allow you to:

- Set daily usage limits for specific apps.
- Schedule downtime where only essential apps are accessible.
- Track screen time reports for awareness.

Example: Limit Instagram to 30 minutes per day. Once the limit is reached, the app locks until the next day.

Step 2: Define Your "Critical Few"

Not every app needs a limit. Focus on the **critical few** that drain time disproportionately: social media, video platforms, and games. Productivity apps rarely require restrictions, but entertainment apps almost always do.

Step 3: Set Limits That Challenge, Not Punish

Too strict and you'll override the limit. Too loose and it won't matter. The sweet spot is a boundary that nudges you without feeling like deprivation. If you spend 3 hours a day on TikTok, cutting to 30 minutes may fail; start with 90, then reduce gradually.

Step 4: Pair with Physical Boundaries

Time limits work best alongside physical boundaries:

- Keep your phone in another room during meals or work.
- Use website blockers (Freedom, Cold Turkey, StayFocusd) for laptop distractions.
- Turn off autoplay on streaming platforms to avoid binge spirals.

This way, when the timer hits, the environment reinforces the choice.

Step 5: Schedule Intentional Use

Instead of sprinkling app use throughout the day, cluster it. For example:

- Check social media once at lunch, once in the evening.
- Watch videos only during a designated break.
- Read news in a single 20-minute session instead of grazing all day.

This converts reactive habits into intentional routines.

Step 6: Track and Adjust

Limits are not static. Review your weekly reports:

- Which apps are slipping through?
- Are you consistently overriding limits?
- Where can you cut further?

Think of this as an experiment. The goal is not arbitrary numbers— it's a balance where technology serves life without consuming it.

The Psychological Payoff

Time limits create freedom, not restriction. When you know you only have 20 minutes to check a feed, you scroll with intention instead of mindless wandering. And when the session ends, you're released back into the real world with clarity and energy intact.

Users who implement limits often report feeling as if they've "added hours back" to their days—not because time expanded, but because distractions shrank.

The Takeaway

Apps and platforms will never set limits for you—they profit from your endless attention. But you can. By using built-in tools, targeting the critical few apps, and combining digital and physical boundaries, you transform your device from a bottomless pit of time into a tool you control.

Time limits are not about restriction; they're about reclaiming your most precious resource—your life hours.

Mindful Use — Turning Technology Into a Choice, Not a Reflex

Decluttering your devices is powerful. But the deepest transformation comes when you change the *relationship* you have with them. Most digital clutter originates not from the tools themselves, but from how unconsciously we use them—checking a phone out of boredom, opening a tab without intention, scrolling without noticing time slip away.

Mindful use is the antidote. It's the practice of making technology a conscious choice, not a reflex. Instead of being pulled by habit and design, you pause, ask what you need, and act with clarity.

Why Mindlessness Is the Default

Our brains are wired for efficiency. Habits allow us to save energy by running behaviors automatically. App designers exploit this by embedding **triggers** (notifications, infinite scroll, autoplay) that bypass reflection and push us into loops. You don't choose to open the feed; your thumb does it before your brain catches up.

Mindful use interrupts that loop. It adds a moment of awareness before action—enough to ask: *Do I really want this right now?*

Step 1: Practice the Pause

Before unlocking your phone or opening an app, stop for two seconds. Ask:

- Why am I reaching for this?
- What do I want to get out of it?
- Is there something better I could do instead?

Often, the pause is enough to redirect from autopilot to intention.

Step 2: Redefine Triggers

Instead of letting external triggers (buzzes, pings) dictate use, set internal ones. For example:

- Open email only at scheduled times.
- Check social media only when you've completed a task.
- Use your phone as a tool (maps, calendar) rather than a filler for silence.

This reframes technology as servant, not master.

Step 3: Savor, Don't Skim

When you do engage, do it fully. If you watch a video, *watch it*—don't half-scroll through comments at the same time. If you message a friend, *be present*—not toggling between apps mid-conversation. Depth replaces fragmentation.

Step 4: Build Mindful Routines

Integrate mindful use into daily rhythms:

- **Morning:** Resist starting the day with a feed. Begin with journaling, stretching, or quiet.

- **Work sessions:** Keep your phone out of reach during focused blocks.
- **Evening:** Set a "digital sunset"—a time when devices go away and offline life begins.

These routines anchor you in presence, not reaction.

Step 5: Notice the Aftereffect

Mindful use isn't just about what happens during digital activity—it's about how you feel after. Ask:

- Do I feel lighter or heavier?
- Energized or drained?
- Informed or overwhelmed?

This reflection trains you to recognize which uses add value and which erode it. Over time, your habits align naturally with what nourishes you.

Step 6: Use Tech to Support Mindfulness

Ironically, the same devices that distract can help you stay grounded if used intentionally. Examples:

- Meditation apps (Headspace, Calm) for structured practice.
- Journaling apps to capture thoughts instead of losing them to scrolling.
- Screen time trackers for honest awareness of your patterns.

The key is not the tool—it's how you frame it.

The Psychological Payoff

When you shift to mindful use, your relationship with technology transforms. You feel less reactive, less restless, less fragmented. Instead of wondering where the last hour went, you finish sessions knowing you chose them. That sense of agency is profoundly freeing.

The Takeaway

Decluttering your digital world gives you space. Mindful use ensures you fill that space with intention. By practicing the pause, redefining triggers, and reflecting on how tech affects you, you move from reflex to choice.

Technology stops being a default escape and becomes what it was always meant to be: a tool for growth, creativity, and connection.

CHAPTER 6

Digital Habits That Stick

Daily Reset Rituals — Protecting Your Digital Clarity

A digital declutter weekend can reset your environment, but without maintenance, clutter creeps back. The truth is: clutter is not a one-time event; it's the result of tiny daily choices. That's why you need **Daily Reset Rituals**—simple practices that keep your digital world light, clean, and aligned.

These rituals are not chores. They're like brushing your teeth: small actions that prevent larger problems. Done consistently, they keep your inbox clear, your desktop calm, and your mind focused.

Why Rituals Work

Habits stick when they're short, repeatable, and tied to existing routines. In behavioral psychology, this is called **habit stacking**— attaching a new action to something you already do. By embedding digital resets into your day, you prevent clutter before it multiplies.

Morning Ritual: Start Clean

How you begin the day sets the tone. Instead of waking up to noise, design your mornings to reinforce clarity.

- **Check, don't scroll.** Look only at essential alerts (messages, calendar) before starting the day. Skip feeds and inboxes.
- **Review your mission.** Glance at your task list or calendar so your day begins with intention.
- **Clear yesterday's leftovers.** If one or two files or messages lingered overnight, resolve them quickly.

This morning ritual ensures you step into the day with focus, not distraction.

Midday Ritual: The Quick Sweep

By midday, clutter begins to accumulate—new emails, stray files, half-open tabs. A five-minute reset restores order.

- **Inbox check.** Process emails quickly using delete, delegate, defer, or respond. Don't let them pile up.
- **Tab check.** Close everything not related to your current task.
- **File check.** Move downloads or working files to their proper folders.

Think of this as a mental stretch break—your brain feels lighter once the small messes are cleared.

Evening Ritual: Shut Down with Intention

How you close the day affects how you rest. Scattered desktops and unread notifications create unfinished loops that your mind carries into sleep.

- **Inbox zero lite.** Get as close to clear as possible so tomorrow starts fresh.
- **Desktop sweep.** Drag loose files into the right folders. Don't leave them floating.
- **Phone reset.** Silence nonessential notifications, and put your device in a charging station away from the bed.

This ritual closes loops so you can disconnect fully, knowing nothing urgent is left undone.

The Weekend Micro-Reset

Beyond daily rituals, a short weekly reset prevents buildup. Dedicate 30 minutes every weekend to:

- Clearing downloads.
- Reviewing cloud sync.
- Updating filters and unsubscribes.
- Tidying your home screen or desktop if clutter has crept back.

This weekly touch-up ensures your system stays strong without requiring another full-scale declutter.

The Psychological Payoff

Rituals do more than prevent clutter—they create rhythm. When your digital life is cleared daily, your mind trusts the system. You no longer carry the subtle weight of *"I'll deal with it later."* Instead, you finish each day with closure, which builds confidence and calm.

The Takeaway

Decluttering once gives relief. Decluttering daily gives freedom. By anchoring quick resets into morning, midday, and evening routines, you protect the clarity you've worked hard to create.

Digital clutter doesn't need to be a recurring problem. With daily rituals, you stop it before it starts—and keep your digital life light, intentional, and aligned with growth.

Weekly Review — Staying Ahead of Digital Clutter

A clean digital environment won't stay clean on its own. New emails arrive, files accumulate, apps update, and notifications slip back into your life. That's why the **Weekly Review** is critical. It's not about perfection—it's about staying ahead of the mess before it becomes overwhelming.

Think of it as digital housekeeping. Just as you wouldn't wait a year to tidy your home, you shouldn't wait months to reset your devices. A short, intentional weekly review ensures your digital life remains light, organized, and functional.

Why a Weekly Review Matters

Psychologists studying attention note that unresolved clutter creates **open loops**—small, lingering reminders of unfinished business. Left unchecked, these loops drain mental energy. A weekly review closes them, restoring focus and calm.

Without a weekly review, clutter slowly rebuilds until you're back where you started. With it, you maintain the benefits of your big declutter weekend with minimal effort.

Step 1: Inbox Sweep

Spend 15 minutes processing your inbox:

- Archive or delete what's no longer relevant.
- Respond to quick messages immediately.
- Move longer tasks into your to-do system.
- Reapply the unsubscribe rule to any new clutter that slipped in.

This prevents your inbox from ever becoming a stress-inducing backlog again.

Step 2: File & Folder Check

Go through your desktop, downloads folder, and cloud drive:

- Move files into their proper folders.
- Delete duplicates and temporary items.
- Rename anything with unclear titles using your naming system.

Five minutes here keeps your storage streamlined and your search effortless.

Step 3: App & Screen Audit

Review your phone's home screen and computer dock:

- Have new apps crept in?
- Are distractions sneaking back onto page one?
- Can you delete or relocate anything to preserve focus?

Small adjustments now prevent another full-scale app audit later.

Step 4: Notifications Check

Open your notification settings:

- Did any apps silently turn alerts back on after an update?
- Are you still getting pings that don't deserve your attention? Re-silencing them ensures your phone stays quiet.

Step 5: Calendar & Task Reset

Look ahead to the week:

- Review your calendar so surprises don't catch you off guard.
- Scan your task manager or notes app, clearing outdated reminders.
- Set priorities for the coming week so your technology supports your goals.

This step turns your digital tools into planning allies, not stressors.

Step 6: Reflection Question

End each review with one question: *What caused the most digital clutter this week, and how can I prevent it next week?*

This keeps your process adaptive. Maybe you notice newsletters creeping back in, or photos piling up. Awareness lets you refine your system week by week.

The Time Commitment

A full weekly review takes **30–45 minutes**. Done consistently, it saves hours of future chaos. The best time? Friday afternoon or Sunday evening—closing one week and preparing for the next.

The Psychological Payoff

People who adopt weekly reviews often describe the shift as *"resetting my brain."* Instead of carrying digital mess into the new week, they start fresh, confident that everything is organized and under control. This ritual transforms technology from a burden into a support system.

The Takeaway

Decluttering once is relief. Daily resets keep the floor clear. But the weekly review is what makes the system sustainable. In less than an hour a week, you preserve the clarity you worked hard to build—and ensure your digital life supports growth instead of sabotaging it.

Boundaries — Protecting Your Time and Attention

Decluttering resets your digital world. But without boundaries, clutter always returns. Every ping, every feed, every "quick check" is an invitation to break focus and fill your mind with noise. Boundaries are what separate the intentional use of technology from its unconscious overuse.

A boundary is not a punishment—it's a line that protects what matters most: your focus, your energy, and your relationships.

Why Boundaries Are Essential

Psychologists studying self-regulation find that **environmental cues often overpower willpower**. In other words, it's not that you're weak—it's that your phone was designed to win. Boundaries remove the endless negotiation of *"Should I check now?"* by replacing it with a clear rule: *"This is when I engage, and this is when I don't."*

Without boundaries, you're always reacting. With them, you regain choice.

Step 1: Define Device-Free Zones

Physical boundaries reduce temptation instantly. Examples:

- **Bedroom:** Keep your phone charging outside at night. Sleep and waking are no longer dominated by screens.
- **Meals:** No devices at the table. Presence becomes the default.
- **Work Blocks:** Phone in another room during deep work sessions.

By linking spaces with behaviors, you reprogram habits at the environmental level.

Step 2: Set Time Boundaries

Not all hours are equal. Boundaries on *when* you use devices are as powerful as where.

- **Morning boundary:** No feeds or inbox until after your first major task.
- **Evening boundary:** Digital sunset—devices away at least an hour before bed.
- **Work boundary:** Email checked at fixed times (e.g., 11 a.m. and 4 p.m.) instead of constantly.

These rules prevent your day from being fractured into micro-interruptions.

Step 3: Separate Work and Personal

Blurring work and personal tech use is a recipe for burnout.
Boundaries restore balance:

- Use separate apps or profiles for work vs. personal accounts.
- Silence work notifications outside of working hours.
- Avoid using personal devices for work tasks whenever
  possible.

This division ensures you can fully rest when it's time to unplug.

Step 4: People Boundaries

Not every digital request deserves your instant response. Boundaries
also involve communication with others.

- Set expectations: let colleagues or friends know your
  response times.
- Use autoresponders: "I check email twice daily. If urgent,
  call."
- Say no to group chats that drain energy but add little value.

Boundaries with people prevent technology from hijacking your time
through social pressure.

Step 5: Emotional Boundaries

Sometimes the hardest boundaries are internal. Technology is often
used to escape boredom, loneliness, or stress. But reaching for your
phone in these moments usually adds clutter, not comfort.

- Practice noticing the urge: *Am I picking this up for purpose,
  or out of habit?*
- Replace reflexes with alternatives: stretch, breathe, step
  outside.

- Accept discomfort instead of reflexively filling it with scrolling.

These boundaries protect your emotional clarity as much as your schedule.

Step 6: Enforce with Systems

Boundaries fail when they rely solely on memory. Use systems that reinforce them:

- App timers to enforce daily limits.
- Website blockers during work hours.
- Physical separation (phone in another room, laptop closed at night).

Systems turn boundaries into reality.

The Psychological Payoff

Boundaries may feel restrictive at first, but the effect is liberation. You reclaim control of your time, reduce anxiety, and create space for deeper focus and connection. Instead of technology dictating your rhythms, you set the rules.

The Takeaway

Digital declutter is not just about deleting and organizing—it's about defending your time and attention with boundaries. By defining device-free zones, setting time rules, separating work from personal, and protecting your emotional space, you build a digital life that supports growth instead of eroding it.

Boundaries are the invisible walls that make freedom possible.

CONCLUSION

Your Digital Freedom Plan — Living With Clarity and Intention

You began this journey with digital clutter: inboxes overflowing, apps multiplying, feeds consuming hours, and notifications chipping away at focus. Step by step, you've cleared the noise. You've unsubscribed, deleted, silenced, renamed, and reorganized. But more importantly, you've learned something deeper: digital clutter isn't just about devices—it's about attention.

Your attention is your most valuable asset. Where it goes, your life follows. The goal of this weekend reset was never minimalism for its own sake. It was freedom—the freedom to focus on what matters, to create without distraction, to connect without interruption, and to live without the constant tug of digital noise.

Now it's time to put it all together into your **Digital Freedom Plan.**

Step 1: Maintain Your Core Habits

The systems you built—Inbox Zero, app audits, notification resets, minimalist home screens, cloud sync, and naming conventions—are not one-time fixes. They are habits to be maintained. Protect them through:

- **Daily resets:** Morning clarity, midday sweeps, evening closures.
- **Weekly reviews:** Inbox sweeps, file tidy-ups, notification checks, calendar resets.
- **Monthly audits:** App pruning, feed reviews, photo/file cleanup.

These small rituals prevent relapse into chaos.

Step 2: Strengthen Your Boundaries

Technology will always push for more of your attention. Your defense is clear boundaries:

- Device-free zones (bedroom, meals, work blocks).
- Time boundaries (digital sunsets, scheduled inbox checks).
- Emotional boundaries (choosing presence over reflex).

Boundaries are not restrictions—they're shields that protect what matters.

Step 3: Redesign Your Relationship With Feeds and Social Media

The feeds will never stop scrolling. The algorithms will never stop recommending. But you have a choice:

- Unfollow aggressively.
- Curate intentional sources.
- Use time limits and batch engagement.

This is how you move from consumption by default to consumption by design.

Step 4: Keep Technology in Its Place

Your devices are tools, not masters. Revisit your **digital mission statement**: a simple line that defines how technology should serve you. Every decision—installing an app, subscribing to a service, responding to a notification—should pass through that filter.

When you live by this, you stop chasing digital efficiency and start living digital clarity.

Step 5: Reinvest Your Freed Time

Decluttering isn't just about less. It's about *more*:

- More deep work.
- More presence in relationships.
- More rest, play, and creative exploration.

What you remove from your digital life is only half the equation. What you add to your real life completes it.

The Takeaway

Your digital freedom plan is simple:

- **Declutter once.**
- **Reset daily.**
- **Review weekly.**
- **Protect with boundaries.**
- **Live intentionally.**

This is not a weekend challenge—it's a lifelong shift. Every step you take away from clutter is a step toward clarity. Every boundary you enforce is a declaration of ownership over your time. Every mindful choice is proof that you are no longer controlled by your devices— you are in control of them.

Digital clutter is the modern enemy of focus, but it is one you can defeat. The tools are in your hands. The freedom is yours to claim.

Your future is not in your feeds. It's in your focus. Choose it. Protect it. Live it.

Thank you

Thank you for choosing to spend your time with this book. In a world full of noise and distraction, your decision to invest in clarity and focus is no small thing. My hope is that the ideas, strategies, and rituals you've practiced here will not just declutter your digital life for a weekend, but transform how you use technology for years to come.

If this book has helped you find calm in the chaos, reclaim your attention, or simply take one step toward living more intentionally, I would be deeply grateful if you shared your experience. The most powerful way you can support this work—and help others discover it—is by leaving a short review on Amazon.

Your feedback matters more than you think. Reviews guide other readers who are searching for the same clarity you've now begun to build. Even a few sentences about what you found useful can make a real difference.

Thank you again for reading, for reflecting, and for doing the hard work of resetting your digital world. The journey toward growth and freedom doesn't end here—it continues every time you choose focus over noise, and intention over habit.

Stay mindful. Stay free. And most importantly, stay in control of your attention.

Eric LeBouthillier

www.ingramcontent.com/pod-product-compliance
Lightning Source LLC
Chambersburg PA
CBHW061715120626
46550CB00003B/1231